W9-COG-578

WITHDRAWN

ELEANOR ROOSEVELT

EQUAL RIGHTS LEADERS

Don McLeese

Publishing LLC
Vero Beach, Florida 32964

© 2003 Rourke Publishing LLC
All rights reserved. No part of this book may be reproduced or utilized in any form or by any means, electronic or mechanical including photocopying, recording, or by any information storage and retrieval system without permission in writing from the publisher.
www.rourkepublishing.com

PHOTO CREDITS:
All photos courtesy of the Franklin D. Roosevelt Presidential Library

Cover Photo: *Eleanor Roosevelt (1884-1962), wife of 32nd President of the United States, Franklin D. Roosevelt.*

EDITOR: Frank Sloan

COVER DESIGN: Nicola Stratford

Library of Congress Cataloging-in-Publication Data

McLeese, Don.
Eleanor Roosevelt / Don McLeese.
p. cm. — (Equal rights leaders)
Includes bibliographical references and index.
Contents: First lady — Eleanor's childhood — Eleanor's father — School in London — Marrying Franklin — Family life — The president's wife — Helping people — First lady of the world.
ISBN 1-58952-289-3
1. Roosevelt, Eleanor, 1884-1962—Juvenile literature. 2. Presidents' spouses—United States—Biography—Juvenile literature. [1. Roosevelt, Eleanor, 1884-1962. 2. First ladies. 3. Women—Biography.] I. Title.

E807.1.R48 M36 2002
973.917'092--dc21 2002002045

Printed in the USA

MP/W

TABLE OF CONTENTS

First Lady

The life of Eleanor Roosevelt is the story of a shy girl who became the most powerful woman in America. As the wife of President Franklin Delano Roosevelt, she was the **First Lady** of the country. She used her power to help women, **African Americans**, and the poor. People around the world loved her.

The First Lady visits a hospital

Eleanor's Childhood

Eleanor was born on October 14, 1884. Her full name was Anna Eleanor Roosevelt. Her parents, Elliott and Anna, were very rich. Eleanor worried that she wasn't pretty. Her beautiful mother called Eleanor "Granny." And her Aunt Corinne called her the family's "ugly duckling." She was closest to her father.

Eleanor with her father and brothers

Eleanor's Father

Her father called Eleanor "Little Nell." His older brother, Theodore, became president in 1901. The Roosevelt family had a lot of money, and they gave some of it to those who didn't. Eleanor often went with her father when he helped others, at hospitals or with poor families. As she grew up, she continued to help.

Eleanor as a young woman

School in London

Eleanor's father died in 1892, and her mother died in 1894. She lived with her grandmother, who was very strict and old-fashioned. When Eleanor was 15, her grandmother sent her to **boarding school** in London, England. She loved it there! Her teacher told this shy girl that she was "a natural born leader."

Eleanor at school in London

Marrying Franklin

When she returned home, she met Franklin Delano Roosevelt at a party. They were distant cousins. Though some of her family worried about how much time she spent helping the poor, Franklin loved her for it. He wrote his mother, "I am the happiest man in the world, also the luckiest." They were married on March 17, 1905.

Franklin and Eleanor married with children

Family Life

Franklin and Eleanor had five children (a sixth died shortly after he was born). During World War I, Eleanor worked for the Red Cross and visited hospitals. She later became a teacher. Her help was even more important to Franklin after he caught a disease called **polio**, which made it hard for him to walk.

Eleanor and Franklin in 1920

The President's Wife

Franklin became **president** in 1933. Eleanor was the first First Lady to give speeches and write a newspaper column. She pushed for rights for women and laws to protect children who were working. She said, "I never wanted to be a president's wife," but she was very good at it.

At home in the White House, 1933

Helping People

Because polio made it hard for Franklin to move around, Eleanor traveled across the country and told the president what she saw. She visited families of coal miners in West Virginia. They had no shoes, and their houses were falling apart. When she told Franklin, he promised to make things better.

Eleanor at a New Jersey housing project

First Lady of the World

After Franklin's death in 1945, President Harry Truman sent Eleanor to lead the **United Nations** Commission on Human Rights. He called her "the First Lady of the World." President John F. Kennedy later invited her to join his Commission on the Status of Women.

Eleanor Roosevelt died on November 7, 1962. She is loved by all who believe in equal rights and helping the poor.

Eleanor and President John F. Kennedy

Important Dates to Remember

1884	Anna Eleanor Roosevelt born on October 14
1892	Eleanor Roosevelt's father dies
1894	Eleanor Roosevelt's mother dies
1905	Eleanor Roosevelt marries Franklin D. Roosevelt
1933	Franklin D. Roosevelt becomes president
1946	Eleanor Roosevelt is named to United Nations Conference on Human Rights
1962	Eleanor Roosevelt dies on November 7

GLOSSARY

African Americans (aff RIH kun uh MARE ih kunz) — black people, Americans whose early relatives came from Africa

boarding school (BORD ing SKOOL) — a school where students live

First Lady (FURST LAY dee) — wife of the president of the United States

polio (POH lee oh) — a disease caused by a virus. Polio makes it hard to walk or move your muscles

president (PREH sih dent) — leader of a country, such as the United States, or of a company or organization

United Nations (yew NITE ed NAY shunz) — an organization with most of the countries in the world, based in New York City

INDEX

Further Reading

Ellwood, Nancy. *Learning about Integrity from the Life of Eleanor Roosevelt.* The Rosen Publishing Group, Incorporated, 1999.
Cooney, Barbara. *Eleanor.* Viking Penguin, 1996.
Winget, Mary. *Eleanor Roosevelt.* The Lerner Publishing Group, 2000.

Websites To Visit

http://www.greatwomen.org/profs/
http://www.geocities.com/collegepark/library/4142

About The Author

Don McLeese is an award-winning journalist whose work has appeared in many newspapers and magazines. He is a frequent contributor to the World Book Encyclopedia. He and his wife, Maria, have two daughters and live in West Des Moines, Iowa.